KU-257-711

This Ladybird Fourth Picture Book has been specially planned to illustrate familiar objects which a child will enjoy recognizing and naming. There is just the right amount of detail in each one to encourage comment and conversation with mother or teacher, who should talk freely about the pictures - thus helping to build up the child's speech vocabulary. Baby-talk should always be avoided.

*The Ladybird Picture Books
are ideally suited for use with
the Ladybird 'Under Five' series—
'Learning with Mother' and its
associated Playbooks.*

A LADYBIRD

Fourth
Picture
Book

by ETHEL and HARRY WINGFIELD

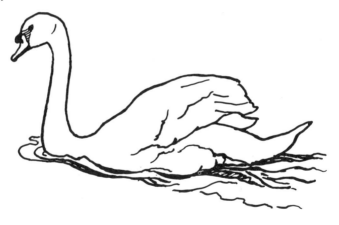

Publishers: Ladybird Books Ltd . Loughborough
© Ladybird Books Ltd (formerly Wills & Hepworth Ltd) 1971
Printed in England

pony

Talking about a pony:

Someone is going to ride this brown pony. It has a saddle for you to sit on, stirrups in which to put your feet, and reins to hold in your hands.
Would you like to ride a pony?

0 7214 0292 5

knitting wool

Talking about knitting:

Are you wearing something which has been knitted?

What colour is it?

Does it feel soft?

What colour is the wool in the picture, and the knitting needles?

toy truck

Talking about a toy truck:

If you had a toy truck what would you put in it?
Have you seen a real tip-up truck?
What was it doing?

holly

Talking about holly:

Holly has spiky, green leaves which can prick
your fingers. What bright red berries it has!

potatoes

Talking about potatoes:

How many potatoes are in the picture?
Do you know how potatoes are made into chips?

swans

Talking about swans:

What long necks these two swans have !
Can you think of any other birds or animals which
have long necks ?

sun glasses

Talking about sunglasses:

Do you know why we wear sunglasses?

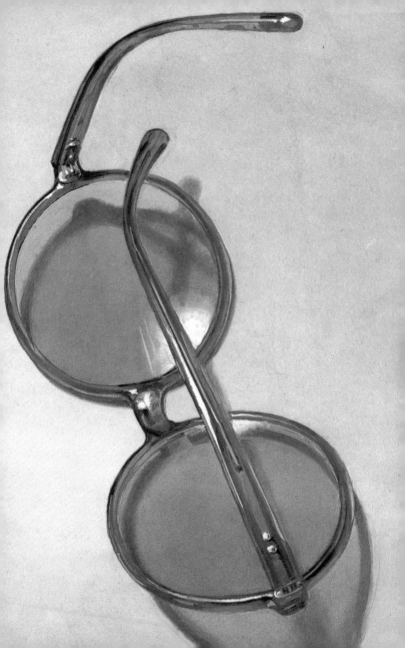

jigsaw puzzle

Talking about a jigsaw puzzle:

What can you see in this jigsaw puzzle?
What kind of puzzles do you have?

hen

Talking about a hen:

Hens lay eggs.
What is this hen going to eat?
She will peck it with her beak.

umbrella

Talking about an umbrella:

This little girl has her umbrella up so she will not get wet in the rain. She will stay dry.
What colour is your mother's umbrella?

paintbox

Talking about a paintbox:

Someone is going to paint a picture.
Can you see the jar of water and the clean sheet
of paper?
What kind of picture would you like to paint?
Which colours would you use?

onions

Talking about onions:

These onions have a brown skin outside and are green and white inside.
What does mother use onions for?
Do onions have a smell?

butterflies

Talking about butterflies:

You can look for butterflies in the garden on warm, sunny days.
Have you ever seen a white butterfly?

puppets

Talking about puppets:

Someone is holding two puppets, one on each hand.

If you were holding them how would you make them move?

What would you make them say?

sheep

Talking about sheep:

Here are some sheep in a field. Some are lying down, one is eating grass, and two sheep are looking for their baby lambs.

pineapple

Talking about a pineapple:

This pineapple will be sweet and juicy to eat. Before we eat it, we have to cut off the outside skin because it is rough.

buttons

Talking about buttons:

Have you any buttons on your clothes ?
What are they for ?
These buttons are different sizes and different
colours. Can you see a red one ?

lamb

Talking about the lamb:

When this baby lamb hears its mother bleating it will run to her.
Can you see the mother sheep on another page?
Can you make a bleating noise?

clothes pegs

Talking about clothes pegs:

Clothes pegs hold washing on the line, so that it will not blow away in the wind.

How many clothes pegs are there in the picture?

mirror

Talking about a mirror:

What do you see when you look into your mirror ?

bicycle

Talking about a bicycle:

Can you ride a bicycle?
You sit on the saddle. Which is the saddle?
You push the pedals with your feet. Can you see
a pedal?
Which is the reflector? It is round and red.

nuts

Talking about nuts:

Do you like to eat nuts?
Most nuts have hard shells. Do you know how to crack them?

tea-pot

Talking about a tea-pot:

What colour is this tea-pot?

The part where the tea comes out is called a spout.

Where does mother pour the water in to make the tea?

skipping rope

Talking about a skipping rope:

Can you skip?
What colours are the handles of this skipping rope?

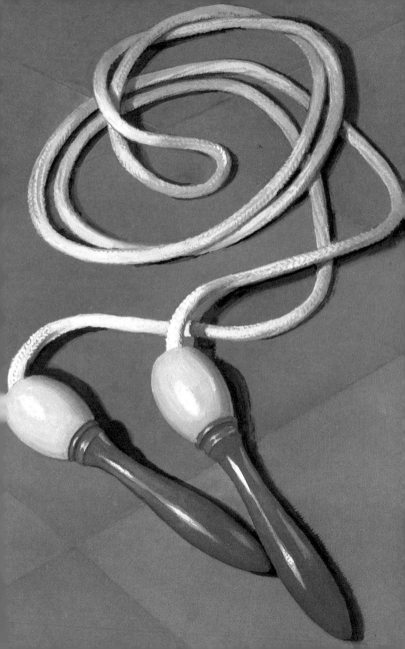

These are in this
and see if you ca